OVERVIEW

Overview

Remember when you were a child and the best toy was a large cardboard box? With a few crayon lines and a wild imagination, that box could become a Roman fort, a family home, a high-rise office, or the vanguard spaceship in an intergalactic fleet. In it, you could go anywhere and be anything. If you were given an empty box to play with today, would you find as many fascinating uses for it as you did back then?

Albert Einstein said imagination is more important than knowledge. He knew it's only through creativity that remarkable things are created. Many people get frustrated because they think "I'm just not a creative person." But everyone has creative potential. Being able to identify and develop the characteristics you already possess can boost your creativity and enhance your creative output in the workplace.

But what exactly is creativity, and how is it linked to innovation? Creativity is the ability to develop something new. It relates specifically to the art of being creative –

seeing things in a new and different way. Innovation is often the end result of being creative. When creative ideas are implemented, this results in innovation.

Creativity

Creativity is evident in the development of original artwork, literature, music, scientific theories, and inventions. In the workplace, brainstorming for new ideas and the development of new products are examples of creativity.

Innovation

Examples of workplace innovation include the introduction of different procedures into a department, using new processes to improve work methods, and the development of new product lines.

Organizations are increasingly turning to creativity and innovation because the ability to develop innovative new products gives a company an advantage over its competitors. And generating ideas for new products – creativity – is the first step in that process.

A creative imagination – just like a healthy body – needs regular attention and exercise. It's easy to get stuck doing what you've always done, thinking the way you always have, and producing what you've always produced.

To break out of the norm, you need to think differently, keep your imagination healthy, and most of all, believe in yourself and your own creativity. In this course, the focus is on enhancing personal creativity so you'll be able to generate creative and innovative ideas. You do this by first assessing your creativity, identifying and overcoming any barriers to creativity, and then by boosting your creativity quotient.

Generating Creative and Innovative Ideas

This course includes strategies to help you recognize how various personal characteristics foster creative ideas at work. Everyone possesses or can nurture these characteristics, which include open- mindedness, making connections, risk-taking, communicating, and persistence. You'll be introduced to techniques to help you recognize and overcome any barriers that limit your creativity, whether the barriers are organizational or personal.

You'll also learn the strategies to enhance creativity, such as thinking outside the confines of the problem or situation, listening to your unconscious mind, using analogies, and drawing ideas from different sources.

Think back to a time when you sat around with coworkers and brainstormed to find ways to address an identified problem or opportunity. As you searched for answers, you might have let your rational, judging mind take a break and instead relied on a more creative, open approach. Perhaps some of the ideas were fanciful or overly ambitious?

But in your brainstorming session, you knew that it's normal for some ideas to stretch the bounds of reality. You and your colleagues may have abandoned some of these fanciful ideas because they were unsuitable. But some ideas, or parts of them, were undoubtedly kept, or they sparked a more suitable idea.

Many of today's most successful businesses are those that have been most creative and therefore innovative. Creativity is a powerful tool for innovation and can drive businesses forward. Embracing and encouraging your organization to be creative can mean the difference between success and failure.

But before putting your ideas into practice, you need to make sure those ideas will work. This course covers three main methods to help ground your ideas in reality.

Using the creative process

Applying a creative process model can help you generate innovative and creative ideas to address the needs of your organization. The creative process balances creativity with analysis to help you generate the best, most appropriate ideas.

Verifying the workability of ideas

One stage of the creative process is verifying the workability of ideas. This stage is pivotal because it's here that you analyze the ideas to ensure they address the identified need and support the organization.

Building on ideas

Building on ideas is something that happens as you work to verify their workability. Like the original ideas, these modifications on ideas must also move through the earlier stages of the creative process before they're verified for workability. The iterative nature of the creative process helps make the best use of its creative and analytical capabilities. This will help you to implement the best idea in the most effective way.

Learning to generate creative ideas will help you, your team, and your organization find better solutions to problems, as well as ways to improve work practices.

CHAPTER 1 - ENHANCING YOUR CREATIVITY

CHAPTER 1 - Enhancing Your Creativity

SECTION 1 - ASSESSING YOUR CREATIVITY

SECTION 1 - Assessing Your Creativity

The characteristics creative people possess are open-mindedness, the ability to make connections, the willingness to take risks, strong communication skills, and old-fashioned persistence. These are the essential attributes for creativity. Technical know-how, the ability to mold ideas into solutions, and analytical skills are also desirable attributes that can help make you more creative.

PERSONAL CHARACTERISTICS FOR CREATIVITY

Personal characteristics for creativity

Have you ever marveled at someone's solution to a problem and thought "I wish I could be that creative"? People wrongly think that creative people are a breed apart, born rebels who think differently and break the mold. In fact, creative people have no more energy than most, are no more confident in general, nor are they introverted hermits who isolate themselves and think only great thoughts. While certain people may be able to use more of their creative skills than others, creativity can be fostered in many ways.

Some people are indeed born with a creative streak. But others become equally successful innovators by making the most of their circumstances and intelligence, and believing in themselves.

In fact, one of the most important traits of creative people is simply that they don't ever doubt their creative abilities. When you have no doubt about your own creativity, creativity will bloom within you.

A constant flow of new ideas is essential for companies to be competitive. To aid in generating ideas, there are some essential personal characteristics that enhance creativity at work:

- Being open-minded means you're open to possibilities and opportunities. After all, ideas don't magically appear; they always build on what came before. Open-minded people give full consideration to ideas that may have been dismissed by others, which may well lead to a new idea.
- Making connections among diverse ideas can help you with synthesis, where two or more existing ideas are combined into a third new idea. Creativity doesn't come with one brilliant flash, but from a reaction between many tiny sparks.
- Being willing to take risks is one of the main ways to find new ideas and innovations. You have to be prepared to push against conventions, challenge others, and do things in a different way. Creative people consider problems and risks to be interesting challenges.
- Possessing strong communication skills is essential for any innovator. You need to be able to communicate your ideas if you want others to collaborate with you. Other people bring new ideas, perspectives, questions, and experiences to whatever you're working on. And when new perspectives come together with your own, the creative sparks often fly.
- Being persistent helps ideas come to fruition. Creative people stick with their ideas and see

them through, even when the going gets tough. Even bad ideas can be useful, since they can make a critical link in the chain that leads to an innovation if you just keep at it.

Open-mindedness is a particularly vital characteristic because it runs through or enables other essential traits for creativity. Being open-minded means you're not limited by assumptions and other restricting beliefs. It makes you curious about your surroundings, receptive to new ideas, and able to examine organizational problems and processes in a different way.

Being open-minded can help you make connections among diverse ideas. Being open to perspectives other than your own allows you to consider ideas from many different sources. A characteristic of creative people is that they can discover and forge the connections among these ideas.

Of course, it's hard to be creative without a critical mass of knowledge related to the particular area in which you work. Especially in an organizational setting, you need more than new perspectives to make connections; you need to have at least some understanding of the area of expertise. Some of the most creative ideas come from those working on a particular project or task every day. Employees often have new ideas on how to make their work easier and more effective.

But expertise in one area has to be balanced with an understanding of other fields in order to make connections. Knowledge and learning can help you build on previous ideas to discover ways to take an idea from one situation and extend it to another. Addressing a demand or need may involve finding the patterns and then creating combinations of ideas. Going beyond current practices to find these connections can make your organization more effective and more competitive.

Being open-minded

The ability to hold off on judging or critiquing an idea is important in the process of creativity. Often great ideas start as crazy ones. If critique is applied too early, the idea will be killed and never develop into something useable.

For example, James is a software programmer who's been thinking about an idea that his coworkers have dismissed as unworkable or outlandish. Because he's open-minded, he doesn't dismiss it, and later bases a database innovation on it.

Making connections

Being able to make connections among diverse ideas can lead to the generation of new, creative ideas. Consider the history of barcodes. The barcode system of product scanning was developed using ideas from Morse code and from optical soundtracks, two widely divergent fields.

Question

Another personal characteristic that enhances creativity is being willing to take risks. Taking risks means daring to try new things with no control over the results or consequences.

Some people are so afraid of risk-taking that their inner critics clamp down just as they begin to explore creative new areas. Does this describe you? How open are you to risk-taking?

Options:

1. I often take risks
2. I like the idea of taking risks but I don't often do so

Generating Creative and Innovative Ideas

3. I don't think risk-taking pays off, so I avoid taking risks

Answer:

Option 1: If you often take risks, that's a characteristic you share with many other creative people. Creative individuals have less fear of making mistakes and social disapproval than the average person. They're strong enough to admit when they're wrong or in trouble, and they analyze and learn from errors.

Option 2: If you hesitate to take risks, you may need to let go of the grand illusions of perfection that typically compensate for the fear of failure or incompetence. Or you may need to establish a support system to help you cope with any fallout from taking risks.

Option 3: Most people avoid taking risks out of a desire for self-preservation. But even if you don't like to take risks, you can try to develop a risk-taking mentality. Remember that so-called "failures" can be channeled into opportunities and experiences that form a springboard for creative thought.

Risk-taking stimulates creativity, because taking chances allows you more freedom to connect and combine seemingly unrelated ideas and activities. This helps you transform the standard way of doing things into something new and original. Of course, risk-taking also relates to being open-minded. You can only come up with new ideas and innovations if you're prepared to push against conventions, challenge others, and do things in a different way.

For example, if you accept some risk on a development project, you'll increase the flow of innovative ideas and therefore test more new solutions. In all probability, many will fail. So the risk is considerably greater than if you choose to play it safe. But there's also a chance some solutions will succeed. And even failed products aren't necessarily damaging to the business, since they can be a source of information and lead to real innovation. Considering all this, it's easy to understand why risks are well worth taking.

Along with taking risks, being skillful at communication allows you to be creative. It enables you to explain and sell your new ideas to others in the company.

Being able to communicate the benefits of a new idea is vital for securing buy-in. Without buy-in from stakeholders, no innovator would get far. There have been many potentially superior products that never made it to market because of their creators' inability to communicate to others why their ideas were good.

In general, social skills have a significant impact on your ability to be creative because they have a big effect on collaboration. Creative people exhibit good team skills through being broadminded, good listeners, and able to develop rapport with others. You will use communication skills as you draw on new ideas from outside your specific area of expertise. You need to build relationships and access the knowledge, skills, and support required for creativity to flourish.

The last personal characteristic for creativity is the attribute of persistence. Many innovators claim that their ideas have succeeded through sheer persistence and tenacity. They refused to let their ideas fizzle out and often kept working away despite reluctance shown by their organizations.

Willing to take risks

Many of the world's top companies were founded by visionaries during recessions. Hewlett-Packard began during the Great Depression, and Microsoft started during the downturn of the 1970s.

Possessing communication skills

The late Steve Jobs, co-founder of Apple Inc., was famous for his attention to detail and his passion for great design. But equally important was his talent for surrounding himself with gifted people and explaining what he wanted. For example, he hired noted industrial designer Jonathan Ive, but it was Jobs' communication skills that allowed him to influence the design of many of Apple's iconic products.

Being persistent

James Dyson built hundreds of prototypes of his bagless vacuum cleaner before he found the right solution. For years he tried unsuccessfully to interest manufacturers in what he called his cyclonic vacuum cleaner. As a last resort, he began producing them himself. After hundreds of prototypes, modifications, and tests, one in four British households now owns a Dyson.

There are other desirable, but not necessarily essential, characteristics for being creative:

- Technical ability often gives a person confidence to experiment "outside of the box," which often generates new ideas. But it's not just the technically gifted who can have creative ideas. You can have insight without this.
- Analytical skills enable you to analyze, not just the big picture, but the individual parts of the whole. Recognizing how each part fits in may help you identify the parts that can be useful in other ways.

Or you might realize how some parts can be changed to get the same result in a different way, or get a different result by changing one or two things.

Sometimes having creative ideas is not enough, because your innovative ideas might not be possible in the context of your organization and it's not likely the idea will ever be implemented. In that case, you need to mold your ideas into solutions. If you have the ability to envision the practical implementation of an idea and shape the idea to better fit the organizational culture, it increases the chances that your idea will be accepted.

For example, you might have a great idea for a new piece of hardware that would make a task quicker and more efficient. But if your department doesn't have the financial resources, it's pretty unlikely the part will ever be produced or procured. With creativity, however, you might shape your idea into something that will work within the budget.

Question

Having communication skills is an essential personal characteristic for creativity. Explaining your idea and its benefits is vital for securing buy-in.

Which statements describe why the other essential characteristics of creative people are important?

Options:

1. Pushing against convention, taking risks, and thinking outside of the box in order to be innovative

2. Considering all ideas fully so you don't dismiss a potentially successful idea too early

Generating Creative and Innovative Ideas

3. Taking ideas from one situation and applying them to another because you recognize a similar pattern or need

4. Refusing to give up on an idea because you believe it's promising

5. Being well versed in organizational standards so you know what's expected of you

6. Understanding how to assess the potential risks of a new idea so you can decide to pursue it or not

Answer:

Option 1: This is a correct option. Having the courage to think differently can spring unexpected ideas and solutions into life. The willingness to take risks is an essential attribute of creative people.

Option 2: This is a correct option. Being open-minded and considering all options fully can help you come up with the right innovative idea.

Option 3: This is a correct option. The ability to make connections among similar items, processes, and principles allows you to create innovative combinations.

Option 4: This is a correct option. Being persistent ensures that good ideas aren't lost, even when they seem unlikely.

Option 5: This is an incorrect option. Knowing what's expected helps with business-as-usual thinking, not creativity.

Option 6: This is an incorrect option. Being willing to take risks, not risk analysis, is the characteristic that will help generate ideas.

SECTION 2 - OVERCOMING BARRIERS TO CREATIVITY

SECTION 2 - Overcoming Barriers to Creativity

External organizational barriers and internal personal barriers can limit your creativity. Organizational barriers relate to people, management, resources, and organizational structure. Personal barriers include being negative, fearing failure, making assumptions, and applying too much logic or analytical thinking. Being able to recognize these barriers, and using strategies to help you overcome them, will help you to unleash your creative power.

BARRIERS TO YOUR CREATIVITY

Barriers to your creativity

Did you ever sit down to write, draw, or problem-solve and couldn't think of a single idea? Maybe you have to write an article, design a house, or solve a stubborn problem that needs an innovative solution, and you can't come up with a thing. An important first step in developing creative ability is to identify any barriers blocking your creative ideas.

There are different types of barriers to creativity. Organizational barriers come from the workplace environment, and personal barriers are those you impose on yourself.

Many corporate executives believe creativity and innovation are the keys to success. But while some companies have been extraordinarily successful at bringing innovative products and services to market, others fail. Even with a commitment to fostering personal creativity in employees, there can still be hurdles. In the workplace, the organizational barriers to personal creativity relate to people, management, resources, organizational culture, and the organizational structure itself. Barriers within an organization can hinder creativity and innovation.

People

The people in an organization may hamper creativity. Some may have created an atmosphere of judgment, and so others do not reveal ideas for fear of being ridiculed or appearing foolish in front of colleagues. Harsh feedback from others can lead to lack of confidence, which can compromise creativity.

Management

How the managers of a company view and respond to creativity and innovation is vital. Some managers may be unwilling to take the initiative or responsibility for implementing creative ideas. If managers don't recognize the importance of creativity, they won't provide the time or challenges needed to develop it. And managers who push employees into being overstressed inhibit the natural thinking process that leads to creative thought.

Resources

Resource limitations may hold back your ability to be creative and innovative. Resources such as labor, equipment, or funds either may not be available, or not sufficient or capable of doing what you intend.

Organizational culture and structure

Working patterns and processes can make it difficult for individuals and teams to be creative. If there's an overconformance with rules and regulations, it leads to a lack of freedom to develop. And too many rules can encourage mental laziness. Sometimes there are physical barriers related to organizational structure as well, as

Generating Creative and Innovative Ideas

when departments that need to work collaboratively are physically separated.

Question

Which examples illustrate organizational barriers to personal creativity?

Options:

1. Coworkers who tend to be judgmental
2. Lack of funds to carry through an idea
3. Emphasis on following rules
4. Managers who don't allow employees sufficient time
5. Managers who don't allow for enough training time
6. Team members who need to collaborate closely are placed in the same work area

Answer:

Option 1: This is a correct option. A coworker with a judgmental attitude is an example of the organizational barrier relating to people.

Option 2: This is a correct option. Lack of sufficient funding is an example of an organizational barrier related to resources.

Option 3: This is a correct option. When an organizational structure and culture has a strong emphasis on following rules, the rigid thinking acts as a barrier to creativity.

Option 4: This is a correct option. Not enough thinking time leads to overstressed employees, which is a management barrier to personal creativity.

Option 5: This is an incorrect option. While insufficient training time may impact technical ability, it isn't a barrier to creativity.

Option 6: This is an incorrect option. In fact, physical proximity can enhance collaboration, which can help spark creativity.

ORGANIZATIONAL BARRIERS TO CREATIVITY

Organizational barriers to creativity

Personal barriers to creativity. Perhaps you listed some or all of the following factors:
- being negative or critical,
- fearing failure,
- making assumptions,
- being too logical or over-analytical.

As you may have noted on the previous page, there are four personal barriers that inhibit creativity:
- Being negative results in hypercriticism of your own ideas. But if you don't let your mind experiment, you won't be able to think of new things.
- Fearing failure leads to less risk-taking. The fear of failure is one of the largest obstacles to creativity.
- Making assumptions and making judgments can get you stuck in certain thinking patterns. These "same as usual" patterns don't lead to innovation.

- Applying too much logic or analytical thinking can lead to an overreliance on information and an inability to run with an idea.

Consider this situation. Four people have been tasked with coming up with an innovative solution to an overcrowding problem in their office. Select the employees to explore how each of them struggles with a personal barrier to creativity.

Joe

Joe told himself "I have no experience doing this, and I don't see any way to fit more people in this space." He cuts himself down more than he builds himself up, and he's always critical of his ideas. When Joe thinks the problem can't be solved, he's exhibiting the personal barrier of being negative.

Annie

Annie thinks of several good ideas, but she shoots them all down before presenting them. She has the notion that there's just one right solution to the problem and is stuck because she can't figure out which it is. She tells herself "I need to get this right or I shouldn't say anything at all." Annie is showing classic signs of the personal barrier of fearing failure.

Boris

Boris had a novel idea for redesigning the office that requires removing the cubicle walls. Boris believes management will never go for an open floor plan, so he doesn't tell anyone his idea, or pursue it further. He's encountering the personal barrier of making assumptions.

Savannah

When she was researching a solution, Savannah found research against open floor plans. She also discovered

Generating Creative and Innovative Ideas

evidence that being in close quarters affects productivity. Savannah found herself unable to progress on any ideas because of the contradictory evidence against every plan. Savannah's personal barrier was applying too much logic, leading to "analysis paralysis."

The biggest barrier of all can be thinking that you're not creative. You need to believe in yourself to be able to let your mind flow freely. You don't have to be an artist or a writer to be an innovator – everyone has creative potential.

Question

Which statements are examples of personal barriers to creativity?

Options:
1. "I don't think this can be resolved."
2. "We need to get this right."
3. "The client will never accept that."
4. "The facts show we're on the wrong track."
5. "I don't think your idea has merit."
6. "We can't continue testing this idea without more funding."

Answer:

Option 1: This is a correct option. Thinking there's no way to resolve a problem is an example of the personal barrier of negativity.

Option 2: This is a correct option. A fear of failure can come from "right-answer syndrome" where you get locked into one way of thinking and don't see the value in failure. This can cause so much stress that your creative juices can't flow.

Option 3: This is a correct option. Making assumptions about what a client would accept will shut down entire avenues of thought.

Option 4: This is a correct option. Applying too much logic or overrelying on data won't let ideas flow freely.

Option 5: This is an incorrect option. You or a coworker being overly judgmental is an organizational barrier to creativity, not a personal barrier.

Option 6: This is an incorrect option. A lack of sufficient funding to test an idea is an organizational barrier, not a personal barrier.

PERSONAL BARRIERS TO CREATIVITY

Personal barriers to creativity

Unless the barriers you face are dealt with effectively, it may be difficult to exhibit dynamism and creativity, and you may feel stifled. You need to use appropriate strategies to overcome barriers to creativity. Strategies will differ, according to the type of barrier you face.

Personal barriers to creativity are usually self-imposed. This is good news, because it means you can do something about them. Every individual has different personal barriers to deal with. And unblocking creativity is not an exact science, so you need to experiment and find techniques that will work for you.

Each personal barrier creates a wall between you and your creativity. Chen is a software engineer who's exploring ways to break through her personal barriers to creative thought.

Being negative

To overcome negativity, stop yourself when you find yourself being negative or self-critical. Redirect your thoughts, try to think of one good thing about an idea, and be aware of what you're thinking. Creativity springs from hopeful speculation, and negativity blocks this kind of attitude. Try to wish, hope, and be optimistic for a better way. In addition, it's important to suspend judgment on yourself and don't dismiss half-formed ideas prematurely.

Chen often belittles her own ideas by thinking that they're stupid and not worthy of mentioning or pursuing. To overcome this, she's trained herself to recognize negative thoughts and to shut them down. "When I start thinking an idea is stupid, I look for the good in it. Then I ask myself, 'OK, now is there an even better way?' I deliberately wish for more – for what's currently unattainable – to optimistically spark my creativity."

Being able to recognize when you're being negative is key to overcoming the negativity barrier. Once it's recognized, you can take steps to overcome it with optimistic and productive thoughts.

Fearing failure

To move beyond a fear of failure, you need to expect that some ideas will fail in the process of learning. It helps to test your ideas out on people, perhaps starting with those people you feel most comfortable with. Then you can gather feedback and make incremental changes. Try to treat any mistakes as experiments that teach you something. Then let your newfound knowledge help you find the best solution.

Chen is afraid that her ideas, if implemented, will fail. She's fearful of the potential results. But she also knows that nothing ventured is nothing gained, and she has tried to change her attitude. "Whenever I start something new, I tell myself that some ideas won't make it, but I can learn from all my ideas – especially those that fail. This gives me the courage to look for some real innovations."

It has been said that "the only thing we have to fear is fear itself." And when it comes to ideas, what's the fear? That your idea won't be accepted? If you make it a point to run your ideas by a trusted colleague, you can give it a trial run in a "safe" environment. That your idea, if implemented, will fail? That's why you seek approval for ideas, especially if there's a cost of some type associated with the failure. Then, if it's approved and fails, at least you're not solely to blame.

Making assumptions

Making assumptions is a personal barrier to creativity that can be hard to recognize. Do you make or hold on to any assumptions that are not necessarily true? One way to overcome making assumptions is to question things. Asking lots of "why?" questions is important in overcoming the tendency toward making assumptions or accepting things as they appear. Another way is to avoid routine by trying something different and changing the way you get information. To really break through the assumptions barrier, you need to expose yourself to diverse stimuli. You can do this by getting other viewpoints.

Chen was asked to come up with some ideas for a new program designed to reduce manufacturing defects on one of the assembly lines. Since she had developed the process using the finest engineering advice available, she made the assumption that the problem must be with the people doing the job.

"I didn't realize I was holding on to some assumptions about a particular program until I read this article in a nontechnical magazine I don't usually even glance at. I realized I'd been getting all my information from a single source." "When I tried to seek out some different viewpoints, I changed my perspective and found out that it was the design of the process that was at fault, not the people involved. Knowing that, I was then able to focus generating ideas on the right problem."

Applying too much logic

Relying only on analytical thinking can block conceptual thinking. Practice divergent thinking to help with "overthinking" or overcoming old patterns. Divergent thinking helps ideas branch out one from the other.

Creativity entails making connections, so try to recognize the role that serendipity plays in helping to bridge distances. Let yourself recognize when divergent thinking strategies turn into happy accidents, such as when a spilled cup of coffee stimulates an idea for a waterproof keyboard. Asking "what if" also helps overcome the logic barrier.

As a logically minded engineer, Chen constantly has to guard against overthinking and overanalyzing. To overcome her "analysis paralysis," she practices divergent thinking. "I try now to use visual thinking to examine everything. When I tie my shoes, I try to envision a way to not have to tie them, and when I take out the garbage, I try and envision a zero-waste society. This gets me making connections I'd never have seen before."

Case Study: Question 1 of 2
Scenario

Now that you've gotten some ideas of how to overcome personal barriers to creativity, try and help Ian, who is struggling to come up with creative ideas for a new product line. He's been working on it most of the morning, and so far has nothing down on paper. Select each question, in order, to help Ian identify and solve any personal barriers he may be encountering.

Question

What statements represent personal barriers to creativity that Ian is facing?

Options:

1. "I don't think I'm creative enough to tackle such a high-visibility project."

2. "If I have too many nonworkable ideas, I'll cause budget problems for my manager."

3. "I always thought customers wouldn't pay more for color choices, but I should rethink that idea."

4. "I'm not going to overanalyze each idea; I'm just going to brainstorm."

Answer:

Option 1: This is a correct option. Personal barriers to creativity include bad thoughts about your own level of creativity. Ian is being negative when he thinks like this.

Option 2: This is a correct option. Worrying about the effects of his mistakes shows Ian is exhibiting the fearing failure barrier to creativity.

Option 3: This is an incorrect option. Rethinking assumptions shows Ian isn't exhibiting the barrier of making assumptions about his customers.

Option 4: This is an incorrect option. Ian is making sure he's not applying too much logic, which excludes imagination and synthesis from thought processes.

Case Study: Question 2 of 2

Match the barriers you've identified in Ian to appropriate solutions for overcoming those barriers.

While all of the solutions might be good approaches for improving creativity, only two will solve the specific barriers Ian is exhibiting, so not all solutions will receive a match.

Options:

A. Being negative
B. Fearing failure

Targets:

1. Ian could tell himself he's more than creative enough for this task

2. Ian could pull some folks from R&D together for a half hour to test his new ideas and document what people say about them

3. Ian could spend more time brainstorming creative solutions

4. Ian could visit the production line at each factory to expose himself to different ideas

Answer:

To overcome the personal barrier of being negative, Ian should rein in negative thoughts and redirect his energies.

To overcome the personal barrier of fearing failure, Ian should experiment with ideas and learn from any mistakes.

Practicing divergent thinking can overcome the barrier of applying too much logic, which isn't one of the barriers in this situation.

Changing the way you get information is a strategy that helps you avoid making assumptions, which isn't one of the barriers Ian is facing.

x   Generating Creative and Innovative Ideas

SECTION 3 - BOOSTING YOUR CREATIVITY QUOTIENT

SECTION 3 - Boosting Your Creativity Quotient

When people are doing work they love, creativity can flourish. And when people feel creative, they're happier, have more confidence, are better problem-solvers, and are more motivated. Creativity is possible for everyone, not just for a few geniuses. Using the techniques of thinking outside the confines of the problem or situation, listening to your unconscious mind, using analogies, and drawing ideas from different sources can give your personal creativity a boost.

CREATIVITY BENEFITS

Creativity benefits

The human inclination for exploration and discovery of new solutions and opportunities is at the heart of creativity. Over generations, this urge has enhanced the human ability to survive in an unpredictable world. But there's a widespread myth that says all creative geniuses are miserable and lonely.

The myth would have you believe that emotional pain spurs creativity, and it's only depressed geniuses who are amazingly original in their thinking. In fact, happiness – not misery – enhances creativity.

In creativity studies, the connection with happiness is noted often. A 2007 Harvard Business School study collected data from people working on creative projects in various industries. Researchers found a direct correlation between the degree of creativity in the participants' solutions and their satisfaction. The correlation was so high, researchers concluded happiness is fundamental to creativity. Creativity makes people happier. And happiness feeds the creativity loop, allowing people to reach higher levels of innovation.

In addition to increased happiness, being creative in the workplace has other benefits:

- creativity gives you confidence, because you feel that you have contributed something of worth and something new,
- creativity enhances your problem-solving abilities because it opens up new ways of analyzing situations, and
- creativity helps improve motivation because you feel more challenged.

Question

What are the benefits of being creative in the workplace?

Options:

1. Feeling happier
2. Gaining confidence
3. Helping solve problems
4. Increasing motivation
5. Improving emotional intelligence 6. Becoming more organized

Answer:

Option 1: This is a correct option. When people have to make an effort – as with a creative challenge – they feel happier and at their best.

Option 2: This is a correct option. Creativity gives you confidence because you feel that you're making contributions that have real value.

Option 3: This is a correct option. Being creative helps you solve problems because it lets you make new connections that open up new possibilities for problems.

Generating Creative and Innovative Ideas

Option 4: This is a correct option. When you feel more challenged and you're coming up with innovative solutions, your motivation gets a big boost.

Option 5: This is an incorrect option. Creativity doesn't have a direct link with emotional intelligence, although being able to communicate your ideas to other people is important.

Option 6: This is an incorrect option. Being organized can sometimes enhance creativity, but other times, randomness can help you to make new mental connections.

ENHANCING CREATIVITY

Enhancing creativity

Just as suffering isn't a precondition for creativity, it's also true that creativity isn't just for a select few geniuses. Creativity is present to varying degrees in virtually everyone. Originality and ingenuity draw on ordinary abilities, such as noticing, remembering, seeing, speaking, hearing, and recognizing analogies. And ordinary people can boost their own creativity.

There are various ways that can help any person to enhance creativity:
- think outside the box – in other words, go beyond the confines of the problem or situation,
- pay attention to your unconscious mind – it generates thoughts, correlations, reactions, and perceptions even when you're not consciously aware of it,
- use analogies – they help you find correlations, agreements, or associations between things that are otherwise different, and

Generating Creative and Innovative Ideas

- draw ideas from different sources – you'll then have the background to help you combine ideas from many areas and relate them to the problem at hand.

THINKING OUTSIDE THE BOX

Thinking outside the box

You've probably heard the expression "thinking outside the box" when creativity and innovation are being discussed in the workplace. The "box" is the normal way of analyzing things or doing things, and includes all the assumptions that almost everyone involved is making. Thinking outside the box applies to going beyond the confines of the problem and restructuring it. Only then can you use creativity to deal with the problem, or approach it from another angle.

Over time – or from lack of practice – you may become unable to reconceptualize problems. Your focus may be fixated on the demands of the task, or on other constraints such as deadlines, lack of resources, or workplace norms. A creative exercise called Scheerer's Nine-Dot Puzzle is a good example of restructuring. It can help you break out of routine patterns of thinking.

To solve the puzzle, draw four continuous straight lines that connect all nine dots. And you have to do it without lifting your pencil from the paper. How did you do?

Generating Creative and Innovative Ideas

People find it hard to solve the Nine-Dot Puzzle, as they nearly always assume that they're not allowed to go outside the confines of the square. They literally don't think outside of the box!

You can do several things to improve your ability to think outside of the confines of the problem or situation:

- Challenge the accepted ideas and your assumptions about them.
- To ensure you define the problem correctly, don't assume that any existing practices, procedures, or theories are absolutely correct.
- Widen your span of relevance by considering how other industries deal with similar problems.
- Be open and prepared to use chance or unpredictable things and events to your advantage.
- Use creative exercises to strengthen the brain and train your divergent or lateral thinking, which is when your thoughts branch out and explore new avenues. Also train your brain with convergent thinking exercises to help you bring bits of information together.

Maria is a computer game designer. She's trying to generate ideas for a whole new game and is attempting to think outside the box.

Challenge the accepted

Maria has an idea that doesn't fit neatly into her company's standard genre of game play, which is a real-time strategy game. On the verge of giving up on her idea, she realizes she's making a big assumption about what the company wants. She works on the idea and presents it to a very enthusiastic reception.

Define the problem

Maria reaches a snag in her game design. She realizes that she needs to take a step back and define the game from the point of view of the player. She asks herself what the player's end goal is, what the obstacles are in reaching that, and what kind of resources the player needs for that to happen. Only then has Maria defined the problem well enough to understand what the game mechanics have to be.

Widen your span of relevance

In developing her idea, Maria reaches a point of "functional fixedness." As the idea originator, she becomes restricted by the demands of the task and her deadlines. To overcome this, she widens her span of relevance by doing nothing more than playing other people's games. She sees how other designers got past similar problems, and she rekindles her joy of gaming as well.

Be open and prepared

Maria has always been interested in marine biology in addition to computer games. One day she's researching seahorses when she realizes that she can use an aspect of their camouflaging techniques in her game. By leaving herself open to chance and being prepared to use noncomputing ideas, she comes up with a real innovation.

Use creative exercises

When Maria hits a roadblock and can't come up with a name for her game, she uses a creative exercise called stream-of-consciousness to generate a list of possibilities. She writes down everything that comes to her mind as quickly as she can for ten minutes. Then she stops and reads over her list. Because she wasn't self-editing as she wrote, she has ideas that are lively, fresh, and fun.

Generating Creative and Innovative Ideas

Question
You're designing a new motorcycle. Which options use the technique of thinking outside the confines of the problem or situation?
Options:
1. Challenging the fact that motorcycles run on gas and have two wheels
2. Taking a magazine and cutting out random words and images, then putting them together in various ways
3. Noticing how others are doing things, and asking yourself how you can apply that to your own problems
4. Riding a motorcycle on a long trip
5. Comparing motorcycles to scooters

Answer:
Option 1: This is a correct option. Challenging the accepted requires identifying assumptions. You don't expect to prove these wrong, but challenging them can lead to creative possibilities. And who knows, maybe the market is ready for an electric three-wheeled motorcycle!

Option 2: This is a correct option. Using creative exercises, such as randomizing words and images, is a way to spark lateral thinking and get you connecting thoughts and ideas in new ways.

Option 3: This is a correct option. Considering how other people and companies do things can help you think outside the box by widening your span of relevance.

Option 4: This is an incorrect option. Riding on a long trip may give you deeper understanding and appreciation for motorcycles, but it won't help you think outside the box.

Option 5: This is an incorrect option. Comparing one similar product to another won't help you think outside the confines of a situation.

USING YOUR UNCONSCIOUS MIND

Using your unconscious mind

Another way to enhance creativity is to pay attention to your unconscious mind. This includes unconscious feelings and thoughts, automatic skills and reactions, unnoticed perceptions, and habits, fears, and concealed desires. To enhance this ability, you need to allow your conscious mind the freedom to create, and don't jump to certainties in the face of ambiguity. You have to give your "deep mind" time to work so creative ideas can "cook" in the back of your mind.

Your unconscious mind is the source of dreams and the random thoughts that appear without apparent cause. It's also where memories are stored that may be forgotten but are still accessible.

It's where implicit knowledge resides, which includes all the things you know so well that you can do them without thinking. But this can only happen when you allow your mind freedom, and don't jump to certainties or conclusions.

Many people have experienced the operation of the unconscious mind. It's what's responsible whenever you wake up in the morning with a new idea that solves the problem you've been struggling with.

When you allow your mind freedom from obligatory, occupational concerns and emotions, it's possible to make unusual connections. History is full of examples of this type of "unconcentration" that provides the right insight into things. Newton lazing under an apple tree and making the connection to the theory of gravity is just one insight that changed the course of science.

Question

Your company is facing a hazardous waste disposal problem. There are many subtle complexities involved, and no one clear solution.

Which are examples of listening to your unconscious mind in this situation?

Options:

1. You create abstract doodles of lifecycles and let your mind flow freely as you draw
2. Although you're sure of the waste tank's limitations, you ignore them as you dream up ideas
3. You research how a company in another country is handling the problem
4. You challenge the fact that the waste is hazardous

Answer:

Option 1: This is a correct option. Allowing your mind freedom to dream can stimulate a new approach. Although you're deliberately not thinking about your subject, you may end up being able to use the drawings as stimuli for a new design.

Generating Creative and Innovative Ideas

Option 2: This is a correct option. If you don't jump to certainties, you can release your unconscious mind. You may even come up with an innovation to improve the waste tank as you solve your disposal problem.

Option 3: This is an incorrect option. Research can stimulate creativity by helping you think outside the box, but it's not a method to listen to your unconscious mind.

Option 4: This is an incorrect option. Challenging the standard way of thinking will help you think outside the box, and it's possible the waste can be broken down or changed into useful or nonhazardous materials. But thinking this way won't help you listen to your unconscious mind.

USING ANALOGIES

Using analogies

Another useful technique to enhance creativity is to use analogies. Analogies show how things that are otherwise different can also be similar, and they can help you understand the basics of a situation quickly. They're useful for explaining, generating, or describing ideas. Analogies improve imaginative thinking because they help you find models or solutions in nature, in existing products or services, or in other organizations. When you seek analogies, it helps make the familiar strange, and the strange familiar.

The word "like" is usually used when making analogies. There's even a common analogy about creativity: that ideas are like light bulbs switching on. Making an analogy might be as simple as saying "This problem seems to be like that one. Maybe we could try our solution to that problem and see where we get." Or you might say a production line backlog is like putting a cork on a high-pressure hose. That comparison immediately shows the energy and danger of the problem.

Generating Creative and Innovative Ideas

Question
You work for a medical supply company, and you're trying to get past a problem with your idea for a new wireless blood pressure monitor. Which are examples of using analogy in this situation?
Options:
1. You think, "the monitor is like a guard dog that will alert its masters to any intruders in the night"
2. You consider that a vehicle dashboard is a good metaphor for a blood pressure monitor since it gathers information from different sources and provides a snapshot of the current situation.
3. You tell yourself, "the brain is like a computer that never needs rebooting"
4. You create drawings of your idea for the battery case in the blood pressure monitor

Answer:

Option 1: This is a correct option. Using an analogy that represents the way blood pressure monitor goes off if the person's blood pressure varies outside the threshold limits will help stimulate ideas.

Option 2: This is a correct option. Analogies give you a framework to understand information, which will help you find solutions. The vehicle dashboard is a good analogy because the blood pressure monitor checks pulse rate, the pressure of the blood when the heart contracts and also the pressure between heart beats to provide a snapshot of the current situation.

Option 3: This is an incorrect option. "The brain is like a computer" is a perfectly valid analogy, but it's not one that will help generate creativity in this situation, since it doesn't tie in the problem at hand – blood pressure monitors.

Option 4: This is an incorrect option. Drawings and schematics are useful in production, but they're not examples of using analogies.

DRAWING IDEAS FROM MANY SOURCES

Drawing ideas from many sources

The final method to enhance creativity is by drawing ideas from many sources. When you sharpen your curiosity and skills of observation, you can collect different points of view from various sources. Appreciate your surroundings and gather inspiration from them, but don't forget to record your ideas and try to make connections among them.

Remember Maria, the computer game designer who needs ideas for a new game? Select each of the techniques that help her if she gets stalled during her design phase for examples of how she draws ideas from many sources.

Sharpen your curiosity

Maria has always been curious about the underwater world. She works hard at getting scuba certified and goes diving, which just sparks her curiosity about more marine systems. And her observations and physical experience give her ideas about how to model diving in a game.

Appreciate your surroundings

Prompted by curiosity, Maria goes scuba diving and is amazed by the interrelationships of the underwater environment. While diving, she gets all sorts of ideas to use to create a computer game.

Record your ideas

Maria has always recorded her ideas in electronic files so she could try to make connections among them. When she uses scuba diving as a source of inspiration, she has to come up with a new system. She records what she sees with an underwater video camera, and then writes in a pocket journal on the boat after the dive. She even e-mails herself a couple of ideas from her cell phone when she's too wet to write things down.

Question

You're an engineer with a large package distribution company. You're trying to come up with innovative ways to plan the distribution routes for the delivery trucks.

Which are examples of drawing ideas from many sources in this situation?

Options:

1. Researching dog rescue web sites, since they often transport animals to foster homes and shelters

2. Researching and watching how bees explore their surroundings but always get directly back to the hive

3. Picking up on the fact that you keep dreaming of trees

4. Questioning assumptions such as "a truck has four wheels"

Answer:

Option 1: This is a correct option. Researching dog rescue sites will help you draw ideas from a completely different source than you'd normally use.

Generating Creative and Innovative Ideas

Option 2: This is a correct option. Sharpening your curiosity and observing your surroundings are ways to draw ideas from more sources than you'd normally encounter at work.

Option 3: This is an incorrect option. Listening to your unconscious mind by noticing recurring symbols can help boost creativity, but it's not an example of drawing ideas from many sources.

Option 4: This is an incorrect option. Questioning assumptions such as "a truck has four wheels" is a way to think outside the box, not to draw ideas from many sources.

No one knows exactly when an "aha!" moment will come to you. You might be formally sitting down to think of ideas, or you might be in the shower. Leave yourself open to ideas from every source available, and be sure to record them so you don't lose any.

CHAPTER 2 - VERIFYING AND BUILDING ON IDEAS

CHAPTER 2 - Verifying and Building on Ideas

SECTION 1 - THE CREATIVE PROCESS

SECTION 1 - The Creative Process

When you want to innovate, solve a problem, or gain improvement, a creative approach can help you develop and implement the best ideas. Creativity can't be taught, but following a five-stage process can help encourage creative thinking.

Once you've identified a need, you begin the process with research and move through several stages: generate ideas, incubate them, verify their workability, and implement them. If you build on your original ideas by generating new ones, you may need to incubate those and verify them in an iterative process that continues until you have a workable idea.

THE CREATIVE PROCESS MODEL

The creative process model

Whether big or small, most organizations are feeling the pressure of heightened competition, in an increasingly global marketplace. More and more, an organization's ability to innovate is key to its success. And you can't innovate effectively without creative people. Facilitating and enhancing creativity throughout your organization will improve its ability to innovate and thereby increase chances of success.

Some people say creativity can't be simplified into a process. However, creative process models do exist and are commonly used in business. Following a creative process model can help you generate and implement creative ideas effectively. Typically, the stages you go through in the creative process are performing research, generating ideas, incubating those ideas, verifying the workability of the ideas, and implementing one or more of them.

Research

Generating Creative and Innovative Ideas

Performing research provides direction for moving forward, helping you to focus your efforts effectively. You need to gather information about the problem or issue to be addressed. You can then determine what information is relevant and useful.

Generate

Drawing on your research, you can generate ideas about how to address the issue or need. You may use a technique like brainstorming to come up with ideas at this stage. You may combine or build on ideas as you generate them, taking into account all the factors that contribute or affect the issue you're addressing.

Incubate

Realistically, not all the ideas you generate will be appropriate. Instead of evaluating them immediately, you should let them incubate – or sit with your subconscious mind. In this way, the ideas will grow or develop as you process them. For example, you may come up with more ideas or find new ways of approaching things. This could lead you in a different direction and to even more helpful ideas.

Verify workability

You begin the critical analysis of your ideas in the verify workability stage. As you verify the workability of a proposed idea, you should focus your efforts on determining which ideas are relevant and useful. At this point, more ideas will likely be generated. This introduces an iterative element to the creative process, where ideas are generated, allowed to incubate, and verified for workability until they're considered workable. Workable ideas are those that achieve the desired outcome, within the contextual constraints of the organization.

Implement

As expected, during the implement stage, you make ideas a reality by putting them into action. This may involve creating a business plan, getting the necessary authorization, gaining commitment from key stakeholders, calculating expenditures, or determining and meeting milestones. You should also consider developing an escape plan – a plan defining when you should, if necessary, abandon implementation.

x

AN EXAMPLE OF THE PROCESS

An example of the process

Jesse is a production line manager at a facility that produces ceramic and earthenware items. The facility is flexible and often fills custom orders. Part of Jesse's job is finding ways to improve efficiency. He wants to come up with a method to speed up production. First, he decides to conduct research.

Jesse begins by carefully reviewing performance reports and statistics. He finds that production turnaround has slowed slightly over the last month. He also talks to workers and supervisors on the production line. From these conversations, he learns that employees are overwhelmed with work at times, but they also experience substantial down time every now and then.

After talking to the floor supervisor, Clarissa, Jesse is more certain than ever that he'll gain efficiencies by improving the process. Clarissa confirms that the production line hasn't been running as smoothly as it should lately. Jesse now feels as though he has enough information to provide direction during idea generation.

Question

Suppose you were in Jesse and Clarissa's situation. How would you go about generating ideas?

Options:

1. Invite knowledgeable stakeholders to participate in a brainstorming session
2. Build on and combine ideas
3. Determine whether the perceived need is genuine
4. Build a model of the production line to help you understand why production has been slowing

Answer:

Option 1: This option is correct. Brainstorming is a great way to encourage the development of creative ideas. Pooling the knowledge of stakeholders helps ensure ideas are useful and relevant.

Option 2: This option is correct. As you search for solutions, you should broaden your scope to include factors that might be contributing to the identified need. To achieve desired results, you may need to address more, or different, things than you originally thought.

Option 3: This option is incorrect. Determining whether the perceived need is genuine is something you should identify at the very start of the process.

Option 4: This option is incorrect. Building a model is a great way to help you understand how the process works. However, you'd probably be better off doing this during the verify workability stage to ensure ideas will address the need.

To help solve the problem with inefficiencies in the production line, Jesse and Clarissa invite some of the best production line workers to a brainstorming session.

Generating Creative and Innovative Ideas

They'll generate ideas about how to speed up production. Contributions center around three main ideas:
- add staff at peak times,
- increase the number of machines working at one time, and
- cross-train employees on multiple stations.

The group generated some good ideas. Jesse is excited and wants to move directly to the verify workability stage.

However, Clarissa insists they step back and let the ideas incubate for a bit. Doing so will give the ideas a chance to grow or develop into more useful, relevant ones. She also argues that a quick, incorrect decision would ultimately be worse than waiting a bit, even if they gain no new insights or thoughts.

After allowing some time for the ideas to incubate, Jesse and Clarissa are ready to move to the next stage. Follow along as Jesse and Clarissa verify the workability of their ideas.

Jesse: Clarissa, I've noticed that production tends to bottleneck at the glazing step. I was thinking we could add more staff at this stage to speed up the process.

Clarissa: Well, Jesse, adding more people would help to get the articles glazed faster. Many hands do make light work, but I don't think it'll address the real problem.

Jesse: Really? Why do you say that?

Clarissa: I've been thinking about it and the problem isn't that the people can't keep up with production. It's that the finishing oven can only produce so many articles. My employees aren't falling behind, the machines are.

Jesse: I didn't realize that. So adding more staff won't help. What about adding more machines?

Clarissa: That won't jive with our budget. Besides, the expense would far outweigh the gains. The articles being produced for a custom order are just too big, and we can't fit enough of them in the oven to keep production flowing. Once the order is filled, the delays should ease up.

Jesse: OK, so adding more machines isn't the solution either. What if we trained all of the employees in all positions? That way, we could float them as necessary. People could move from area to area as needed to move work along in the most efficient manner. Like when only a few items need to be glazed, some people can perform other work. This would address the problem we're facing and prevent similar problems in the future.

Clarissa: That sounds reasonable. But what if we just started with select employees for the time being? That way we can manage the expense of training them and test out how the new process is going to work.

Jesse: I see the value in that idea too. Let's sleep on it and meet again on Friday to discuss it.

When verifying the workability of their previously generated ideas, Jesse and Clarissa built on the idea of training all employees in all positions. Clarissa suggested they first train only a select group of employees, which would build on the original idea and thus return them to the generate stage. Jesse and Clarissa may come up with other ideas during the verify stage. If so, they may incubate and verify those ideas too. This iterative process will continue until they're satisfied an idea is workable, or they find the idea isn't feasible.

Generating Creative and Innovative Ideas

After letting the new idea for training workers incubate, Clarissa and Jesse meet again to verify its workability. Follow along to learn how they made out.

Clarissa: I think hand selecting certain employees to train is the best idea we've had and is the most appropriate solution to our need to improve the efficiency of the process.

Jesse: I've been thinking it over and I agree. We can implement this idea without straining our budget, and it's in line with the organization's mission statement.

Clarissa: So we agree. Shall we move on to implementation?

Jesse: Yes, I agree. I'll start by getting stakeholder commitment. Can you work to create a training plan? And together we can select the employees to train first.

Clarissa: That sounds good. I'll get to work on the training plan right away.

Because Clarissa and Jesse agree that the idea is workable, the process is complete. Now they can move on with implementation, knowing they have a workable idea that will address the problem and support the organization.

Question

Match each stage of the creative process to the statement describing its purpose.

Options:
A. Research
B. Generate
C. Incubate
D. Verify workability
E. Implement

Targets:

1. This stage provides direction for your creative efforts
2. During this stage, you may brainstorm to find potential solutions to a problem
3. It's during this stage that you take a break from thinking about the issue at hand and allow ideas to sink into your subconscious mind
4. During this stage, you determine if the ideas you've generated will work as intended
5. It's during this stage that you make your idea a reality by doing what needs to be done to put the idea into practice

Answer:

Research gives direction to your creative endeavors. It helps you focus your efforts appropriately so you don't waste time and resources.

During the generate stage, you search for ways to solve the identified need. You may come up with many ideas and alternatives at this point.

During the incubate stage, you take a break from idea generation and let the mysterious creativity of the subconscious mind work on the issue at hand. This also helps you avoid hastily implementing ill-conceived ideas or missing a better idea.

For an idea to be workable, it must address the original problem or need. This includes meeting organizational constraints such as company goals and budget considerations.

Implementation is the final stage of the creative process, the purpose of which is to put the idea into practice.

SECTION 2 - VERIFYING THE WORKABILITY OF CREATIVE IDEAS

SECTION 2 - Verifying the Workability of Creative Ideas

Verifying the workability of ideas helps you improve on proposed ideas so they're practical and workable in the context of the organization. When you verify an idea, you draw more on logic and practicality than imagination. And you need to describe ideas in more detail so they can be clearly assessed for workability. Two methods of verifying the workability of ideas are canvassing the opinions of key people and using simulations.

THE VERIFY WORKABILITY STAGE

The verify workability stage

Sometimes ideas fail – it happens. Failed ideas have some things in common: they waste money, time, and resources.

While failure by trial and error may lead to eventual success, you can give yourself a solid foundation for success by taking the time to verify the workability of ideas before you implement them. The benefit is that you avoid wasting time and money on unsuitable ideas.

After you generate ideas, you need to verify them. And the first part of the verification process is to establish whether an idea meets the two criteria for workability:

- it addresses the identified need, and
- it supports organizational goals.

The second criterion – that the idea supports organizational goals – is especially important. For an idea to work in the context of an organization, it should support organizational realities such as budget, mission, and capabilities.

Generating Creative and Innovative Ideas

In the process of verifying the workability of an idea, you'll also need to describe the idea in more detail. You could begin by pointing to what makes the idea unique. You'll also need to describe the benefits and risks, or any obstacles associated with the idea. And you should provide a rough cost estimate for implementation of the idea.

Benefits and risks

You analyze the benefits and risks to determine if the benefits of implementing an idea outweigh any risks it presents. You can use what you learn to take steps to minimize the risks, maximize the benefits, or abandon the idea, if necessary. You might simply list and compare the benefits and risks, or undertake a complex analysis.

Obstacles

It's important to identify potential obstacles that may have a negative impact on the implementation of your plan. Then you can prepare a plan to overcome the obstacles. Examples of obstacles include failing to get approval, insufficient funding, or unacceptable risk.

Rough cost estimate

You should calculate a rough cost estimate of what it will take to implement your idea. In addition to providing the costs, include the projected income that will be generated over time from implementing the idea.

The benefit of checking costs, benefits, and risks is that it will help you implement the idea in the best way. The creative process relies on imagination and creativity to generate ideas. However, because the goal of the process is to implement ideas – making them reality – you need to be certain that ideas will be workable. Critical evaluation during the verify workability stage relies more on logic and practicality than imagination. It's at the verifying stage that the practical-mindedness that comes from critical evaluation is important.

Suppose you've come up with an idea – a way to change a product so that it's completely recyclable. You need to verify the workability of the idea, and in so doing, you build on it.

Verify workability of ideas

Making the product completely recyclable would require the total redesign of the production processes, which is a costly endeavor that your company isn't prepared to take on. Still, because your company has set long-term sustainability goals, this idea has the potential to be workable.

Build-on

Because the idea is too costly for the organization to take on, you build on the idea, reworking it so that only part of the product is made recyclable. This requires only minor alterations to the production processes.

You also develop a plan to make the product completely recyclable in a number of stages, over the course of several years. This will spread out the costs and makes the idea workable in the context of the organization while addressing the originally identified need.

The recycling example demonstrates the iteration that can occur during the creative process. The original idea was built on to make it truly workable.

Question

What are some of the benefits of knowing whether your ideas are workable?

Options:

Generating Creative and Innovative Ideas

1. Helps you avoid wasting time and money on ideas that aren't suitable
2. Helps you implement ideas in the most effective way
3. Helps you prioritize ideas
4. Helps you generate ideas more effectively

Answer:

Option 1: This option is correct. Taking the time to ensure your ideas are grounded in reality will save time and money because it helps you avoid implementing unsuitable ideas.

Option 2: This option is correct. When you evaluate your ideas, you'll increase the chances of implementing them in the most effective way. You can determine the idea's risks and benefits, its obstacles, and its costs, and then base your implementation on this information.

Option 3: This option is incorrect. When you assess whether ideas are workable, you focus on their relevance and practicality. At this stage, you've already established that these ideas are the most important. Typically, you prioritize ideas in the generate ideas stage of the creative process.

Option 4: This option is incorrect. Knowing that your ideas are workable won't help you generate ideas more effectively. When you generate ideas, which occurs before you check their workability, you need to draw on relevant research. Using techniques such as brainstorming can make idea generation more effective.

Question

Which statements describe the purpose and activities of the verify workability stage of the creative process?

Options:

1. You scrutinize ideas from a predominately logical and practical perspective

2. You describe the idea in more detail by creating a rough cost estimate for implementing the idea

3. You check ideas to make sure they will resolve the identified need and support organizational goals

4. You use the brainstorming technique to develop potential ideas to address the identified need

5. You set ideas aside for a while so you can return to them with a fresh mind

Answer:

Option 1: This option is correct. During the verify workability stage, you're focused on checking your ideas to ensure they're workable. This requires more of a logical and practical perspective, rather than an imaginative one.

Option 2: This option is correct. Take the time to investigate the rough costs of implementing your idea to ensure its associated costs aren't prohibitive. This is part of describing the idea in more detail and is one of the activities completed during the verify workability stage.

Option 3: This option is correct. It's essential to check all ideas to ensure they'll indeed resolve the identified need and align with organizational goals.

Option 4: This option is incorrect. You may generate ideas by brainstorming, but this doesn't happen in the verify workability stage. It occurs during the generate stage of the creative process.

Option 5: This option is incorrect. Setting ideas aside so you can return to them with a fresh mind refers to the act of letting ideas incubate. After you let the ideas incubate, you check their workability.

WAYS OF VERIFYING IDEAS

Ways of verifying ideas

Now that you understand the purpose and activities associated with the verify workability stage, you can move on to explore ways to carry out this stage. Various methods exist for verifying the workability of ideas. One is to canvass the opinions of key people. Another is to use simulations. The choice of method depends on the situation. When canvassing opinions, you should discuss the idea with as many people as possible to learn what they think.

For example, you might talk to consumers, colleagues, product developers, marketers, and any other stakeholder you have access to.

Question

How do you think discussing the idea with key people can help?

Options:

1. It can improve on the idea
2. It can build support for the idea

3. It can help improve the research for the issue or problem

4. It can ensure the idea will be implemented

Answer:

Option 1: This is a correct option. Applying what you learn from canvassing can improve the idea, making it more realistic, useful, and relevant in its practical application.

Option 2: This option is correct. Canvassing for opinions helps to build stakeholder support, which improves acceptance and overall effectiveness of the idea.

Option 3: This option is incorrect. Research is typically the first stage in the creative process and occurs before you canvass opinions.

Option 4: This is an incorrect option. After canvassing the opinions of key people, you many find that the idea isn't really suitable. Therefore, the idea may or may not be implemented.

So canvassing the opinions of others can help build on and improve an idea. Getting different perspectives on an idea often helps to refine the idea and make it more practical. Canvassing can also build support for the idea. You can also use simulations to verify the workability of ideas.

Simulations help you gather information, which may generate new, better ideas, and ultimately, ground ideas in reality, making them more workable. A simulation may be a prototype of a new engine, a mock-up of a proposed print advertisement, or a computer model used to understand financial information, or it may be the layout of a specific area of your organization. You can even simulate a process to better understand it.

Generating Creative and Innovative Ideas

Time and money are always important criteria in the decision of which method to use. Usually, canvassing opinions is the best place to start because it's relatively inexpensive and can be done quickly. And canvassing opinions can be particularly appropriate in certain situations. Follow along to explore the circumstances when canvassing is the best method for verifying the workability of an idea.

Resistance is expected: If you have reason to expect resistance from stakeholders, then canvassing for opinions will help you understand the reasons for the resistance and how much resistance actually exists.

Approval is needed: If you need key people to approve an idea in order to keep the idea from being abandoned, then canvassing for opinions may be critical. Finding out why these key people object and then how to gain their approval is essential to the workability of your idea.

Input from many is needed: If you know the idea's success depends on the input of many people, then canvassing allows you to talk to these people to learn about their attitudes and feelings, and gain useful insight and knowledge.

You can also use criteria to help decide when to use simulations to verify workability. Use simulations when aesthetics are important, when you're examining a process, or when there are complex technical details to consider.

When aesthetics are important

Use a simulation when the aesthetic features of your idea are important to assess and stakeholders may benefit from visual presentation of the information. A simulation can help you explore, address, and express important features, attributes, or details. An example may be the design of a cell phone that has two small screens instead of one.

When you're examining a process

Consider using a simulation when you're examining processes. A simulation can help you better understand how a process does or doesn't work. This could be a process such as sales or manufacturing a product.

When there are complex technical details

If the idea involves complex technical details that must be understood, a simulation may be a good choice. A simulation can help you and others understand the complexities of the idea – for instance, when you need to explain a procedure for space shuttle repair.

Question

Here's a chance to practice whether you recognize when to use each of the methods for verifying the workability of an idea. Match each method to criteria that apply to it. You may use each method more than once.

Options:

A. Canvassing the opinions of key people
B. Simulations

Targets:

1. Stakeholders are expected to be resistant
2. Disapproval from key stakeholders will sink the idea
3. Approval of aesthetic features of your idea must be demonstrated in order to gain support
4. Support depends on the understanding of a process

Answer:

Canvassing for opinions can help you learn about stakeholder resistance. In this way, you can address any

Generating Creative and Innovative Ideas

issues stakeholders may have before implementing an idea.

Canvassing can help you build support for your idea. If key people need to approve an idea, finding out what they think about it first can be critical. Their responses can help you improve the idea and get their approval in the end.

Sometimes how an idea will look once implemented is more important than other details. When this is the case, use a simulation to visually describe your idea.

Simulations can be very effective in demonstrating how processes will really work, highlighting things you may have overlooked or didn't realize.

The following example provides an opportunity for you to explore how you'd weigh the two methods in a real-life scenario. A product development team at an automobile manufacturer wants to appeal to a younger market with an SUV hybrid. The average age of the buyer of its current product line is 62, and the team is hesitant about being able to entice younger buyers.

Should the team create a simulation – in this case, a prototype of the new vehicle – or canvass for opinions?

Certainly a prototype of the vehicle would be useful in the design stages of product development. It would help everyone involved with creating the SUV visualize it, but creating one would be costly. And then what if the consumer doesn't want a hybrid SUV like the one the team has in mind?

So how about canvassing for opinions? Asking the targeted consumers what they think of the new model would bring valuable insight about its workability. And because the team already anticipates some resistance, merely because the target audience isn't the company's typical customer, getting opinions may reveal any issues or resistance to the new model.

The team should consider talking to designers, marketers, and industry experts. Moving ahead with a design that doesn't appeal to the targeted consumers, or a design that the company can't feasibly produce, would be a waste of time and money. Canvassing for opinions makes a lot of sense in this situation. Success depends on the opinion of the consumers, and if the idea fails to get their approval, management won't support it either.

This situation may even meet the final criterion because input from many people is required to achieve success. For example, the team will need input from those involved in designing, building, and marketing the vehicle. On the other hand, designing a prototype of the SUV may help consumers envision the new model, allowing them to approve or disapprove of the aesthetic features of the vehicle.

While this is very important when marketing a vehicle, the risk is too great. If the team builds an expensive prototype and then finds out that nobody likes it, a lot of time and money will have been wasted. As such, to verify the workability of the idea, canvassing the opinion of key people is the best option. This idea meets all three of the criteria for choosing this method, whereas it only meets one of the criteria for choosing a prototype.

You need to determine which method to use to verify the workability of an idea. Sometimes using a simulation will be necessary, but other times canvassing the opinions of key people is the best choice.

Case Study: Question 1 of 2

Generating Creative and Innovative Ideas

Scenario

A government agency responsible for providing various services has come up with an idea to reduce costs by changing the process for serving customers.

This change will affect how customer service representatives in several different areas do their job. It's not a complex change, but it will require some extra work on the part of the representatives. The company is expecting some resistance.

Help the agency choose the best method to use to verify the workability of its idea by answering the questions in order.

Question:

How should the agency go about verifying the workability of this idea?

Options:

1. Canvass for opinions
2. Use a simulation

Answer:

Option 1: This is the correct option. Canvassing the opinions of customer service representatives can help build on and improve this idea. Their input will help refine the idea and make it more workable.

Option 2: This option is incorrect. Simulations are used to better understand and visualize how a process might work. However, in this case, the change isn't complex enough to require the use of a simulation. The customer service representatives are a better source of input.

Case Study: Question 2 of 2

Why is canvassing the best method for verifying the workability of this idea?

Options:

1. Because resistance from customer service representatives is expected
2. Because the approval of customer service representatives is critical to the idea's success
3. Because aesthetic features are an important factor in the redesign of the process
4. Because the change involves complex technical details

Answer:

Option 1: This option is correct. In cases where resistance is expected, canvassing is an appropriate method to use. You need to find out what kinds of issues the representatives find most troublesome about the process. This will help improve on the idea to make it more acceptable.

Option 2: This option is correct. The approval of the customer service representatives is essential to success here. This factor on its own makes canvassing the best method to use. The representatives know the process well, and if they don't approve of the change because it's not workable from their perspective, the idea won't succeed.

Option 3: This option is incorrect. Aesthetics apply more to the design of products or other physical objects.

Option 4: This option is incorrect. Describing or exploring complex technical details is a better approach when your idea involves technically complex information. The new process doesn't involve this type of information.

SECTION 3 - BUILDING ON IDEAS

SECTION 3 - Building on Ideas

Naturally, during the creative process, ideas change and grow as they're improved on. Each modification to an idea is considered a build. Like the original idea, a build needs to be evaluated to determine its effectiveness. To be effective, a build must meet certain criteria. A build must be grounded in reality, extend the original idea in some way, and be feasible in the context of the organization.

WHY BUILDING ON IDEAS IS IMPORTANT

Why building on ideas is important

Imagine you're a time traveler. And suppose you land in 1908, just in time to witness the first Model T Ford roll off the production line. Now imagine you jump ahead a few decades to witness a luxury sedan or truck roll off Ford's production line. This imaginary journey highlights how successive, creative innovations can improve an original idea.

The creative process is iterative in nature. As ideas are evaluated, new ideas that improve on the original one are often developed. You build on ideas as you find out more information – for example that an idea will be costly in its implementation or that people in the organization disagree with aspects of the idea. Building on ideas is important because it can result in clearer, more useful, feasible, and relevant ideas. This in turn makes for better results when the final idea is implemented.

Generating Creative and Innovative Ideas

Typically, you start with an idea, build on this original idea, modify that build, and continue modifying until no more improvements are suggested.

Start with an idea

The idea you start with will be one that comes out of the generate stage. This is considered the original idea. For example, a publishing company might have an idea to promote its new poetry series through advertisements in literary magazines.

Build on original idea

During the verify workability stage, you or one of your colleagues may suggest a way to modify the original idea to improve it. For example, the idea to promote a new poetry series by advertising it in literary magazines might be built on with the suggestion for a focused, direct marketing campaign to teachers across the country.

Modify that build

The build may be modified again to further improve the idea. This continues until there are no more suggestions for improving the idea and a final idea is agreed on. Finally, the idea to promote the new poetry series by advertising in literary magazines and direct marketing to teachers may be built on again, perhaps to also include advertising in university papers.

You can make incremental improvements to an idea, or you can combine two or more existing ideas. Incremental improvements to an idea may be necessary if an idea is too big to implement at one time. This idea of incremental improvements ties in with the Kaizen method. Kaizen is a business strategy and philosophy that encourages continuous improvement by asking everyone within an organization to seek ways to improve the way they do business.

Because Kaizen offers a way to make incremental changes, it allows you to build on ideas that aren't yet possible, instead of dismissing them.

You may also find it appropriate to combine two or more existing ideas. For example, suppose you're an engineer working with a team to improve the safety of small cars. Several ideas are being considered for implementation. The first is to add extra crumple zones under the hood. The second is to include a collapsible design for under-hood components. And the final idea is to add additional air bags.

After some discussion, the team decides that the under-hood safety features are too important not to implement and opts to combine them into one. The team will move ahead with implementation of collapsible components and crumple zones.

WHY INCUBATION IS IMPORTANT

Why incubation is important

There can sometimes be a temptation to accept ideas as complete, before they have been thought through. Often, time pressures can lead to the hasty acceptance of an idea. Following a creative process model can help you avoid this. And remember, it's important to sit on an idea for a while – let it incubate – because when you do this, new options or insights may emerge.

The power of incubation is exemplified in the story of how Elias Howe beat Singer to the patent for the sewing machine. His original idea, like Singer's, was to leave the hole at the head, but this wouldn't work. As he struggled to find a solution, Howe dreamed that he was in the jungle, surrounded by natives holding spears with holes at the tip. This gave him the idea to place the hole of the sewing machine needle at the tip instead of at the head, allowing him to solve the problem of how to thread a sewing machine needle.

So forcing yourself to take time out from trying to solve a problem can have its advantages. Our minds need a break from active, purposeful thinking. Have you ever worked on a puzzle for so long that you began to wonder if your efforts were doing more harm than good? Yet after some time away, you return to quickly solve the puzzle you've been struggling with?

While you were busy doing other things, your subconscious mind continued to work on solving the puzzle. The same is true for all situations. Often, an answer or solution will present itself while you're performing a less mentally demanding task, such as walking, showering, driving, or even sleeping, as in Elias Howe's case.

EVALUATING THE EFFECTIVENESS OF BUILDS

Evaluating the effectiveness of builds

As you're thinking about and building on an idea, it's important to ask questions related to that idea – for example: How feasible is it? Does it require too many resources? How would it work in practice?

The objective is not only to improve the original idea so it more effectively addresses the problem or opportunity, but also to make sure the idea supports organizational goals and strategy. So the criteria for an effective build are that it's grounded in reality, it extends or shapes the original idea, and it's feasible in the context of the organization.

You need to evaluate an idea to make sure it's grounded in reality. First, is the build relevant? You should make sure it addresses the targeted problem or opportunity. If it doesn't, it may be a really great idea but actually irrelevant. Another important question to answer to help make sure the idea is grounded is "Does it clarify the idea?"

Suppose you work for a sporting goods company and have an idea for improving the ergonomics of the company's water bottles. You know that anything that will require too much research and development will not be approved. You also know the company has just developed new cushioning material for its line of tennis rackets. You put forth the idea of carving an ergonomic hand grip into the bottle. The team working with you comes up with two builds on the idea – one is appropriate but the other isn't.

Appropriate

Instead of just adding the hand grip, a team member suggests putting a hole through the bottle, allowing a natural grip, and adding antimicrobial cushioning. This is an appropriate build because it's grounded in reality and addresses the targeted problem or opportunity.

Inappropriate

Instead of adding an ergonomic grip, a team member suggests designing a whole new straw-fed water system. The water would be held in a backpack instead of a bottle to make the bottle "hands-free." This is an inappropriate build because it doesn't address the original idea – that of improving the bottle's ergonomics. Instead, it replaces the original idea.

Another criterion for builds is that they extend or shape the original idea in some way. You make the idea better in some way – more profitable, effective, or efficient.

For example, in the case of the water bottle, an appropriate build is one that asks for slip-resistant, absorbent, and antimicrobial cushioning where the bottle is held. The build makes the idea more ergonomic and also more practical because it will help to reduce the effects of sweaty hands and odor.

Generating Creative and Innovative Ideas

Designing a new water system is inappropriate because it abandons the original idea in favor of a totally new idea. While it might be a great idea, it does not extend or shape the original idea in a useful, effective way.

Finally, you must make sure that a build on an idea is feasible in the context of the organization. A feasible build is financially viable, the resources to implement it are available, and it aligns with organizational strategy.

In the water bottle example, the build to put a hole through the bottle and cushion it with a slip-resistant, antimicrobial material aligns with the company's development of cushioning material for use on its tennis rackets.

But the idea to develop a new water system is inappropriate in the context of the organization. It's not feasible because the company would have to develop new technology and rely on resources it doesn't have.

Depending on the circumstances, the questions you ask to determine whether a build aligns with organizational strategy will vary. However, some typical questions can be applied to most any situation:

- How can we test the idea?
- Is the idea unique?
- Do we have a customer base that wants the product or service that'll be generated by the idea?
- Who will we need to implement the idea?
- What resources do we need?
- How much will it cost to implement the idea?

Answering these questions may take the idea in a new direction, improve on an original idea, or make it clearer or more feasible. This will restart the iterative portion of the creative process. And this will continue until no more effective builds are generated for the idea being evaluated.

Question

A manufacturer of personal hygiene products wants to find ways to reduce its reliance on plastic. One idea is to package deodorant in a cardboard container with just the twister, protective seal, and cap being made of plastic. A colleague suggests a build on this idea – that the container be a sealed, peelable container, eliminating the need for any plastic. What questions might you ask to evaluate the effectiveness of the suggested build on the idea?

Options:

1. Do we have the capability to do this?
2. Will it address the problem?
3. Will it make the original idea more effective?
4. Does the build extend the original idea?
5. Does the build clarify the original idea?
6. Why do we want to reduce our reliance on plastic?
7. Is changing from plastic really going to make a difference to the environment?

Answer:

Option 1: This option is correct. The answer to this question will help to determine if the build on the original idea is feasible within the context of the organization.

Option 2: This option is correct. This question will help you to determine if the idea is grounded in reality.

Option 3: This option is correct. This question will help you to determine if the idea shapes the original idea in some way.

Option 4: This option is correct. This question will help you to determine if the idea extends the original idea.

Option 5: This option is correct. This question will help to determine if the idea is grounded in reality.

Option 6: This option is incorrect. This is a question that would have been answered long before now and has no relevance to the build on the original idea.

Option 7: This option is incorrect. This question doesn't help to determine the effectiveness of the build on the original idea. It's really something that would have been considered before the idea was proposed.

FINDING THE BEST BUILD ON AN IDEA

Finding the best build on an idea

Now that you're armed with criteria for an effective build, follow along as a team uses the criteria to evaluate proposed builds on an idea. The Service Department at a car dealership is tireless in its pursuit of great customer service. It sets aside a substantial budget for improvement. For instance, it has just invested in a new database, which can be integrated with Web services. The system is easy to use, and all service personnel are trained to use it.

Customers have indicated that efficiency and timing in making appointments is important to them. One service representative has the idea to add an option to book service appointments via e-mail because of its efficiency and convenience. Other team members suggest builds on the original idea. Follow along to find out what other builds are suggested.

Jan: The idea we are considering is to add e-mail as a contact option for booking service calls. Does anyone have anything to add?

Generating Creative and Innovative Ideas

Dragomir: I was thinking perhaps we could also call people to remind them of recommended services. We'd set up alerts that would prompt us to call customers.

Ella: I have an idea too. What if we add to this an online account for our customers? We could make use of our powerful new database to make available a history of services performed, recommended maintenance, and e-mail alerts inviting them to schedule the necessary appointments.

Fiona: Those are interesting ideas. I thought maybe we could hire a customer service provider to handle the booking of routine service calls. That way we could focus our attention on the customers with more complex issues.

Case Study: Question 1 of 2
Scenario

Now that the service representatives have presented their ideas about how to improve the original idea, they need to evaluate the effectiveness of those proposed builds. Access the learning aid Service Department's Ideas to review the information about the team's proposed builds on the original idea. Help the team evaluate the effectiveness of the proposed builds to determine the best one. Answer the questions in order.

Question

Which of the team member's ideas is the best build on the original idea?

Options:

1. Add online accounts for customers
2. Set up alerts to call customers
3. Hire a provider to handle routine service calls

Answer:

Option 1: This is the correct option. Ella's suggestion expands on the original idea and makes good use of company resources.

Option 2: This option is incorrect. Dragomir's build isn't the most effective because it moves away from the online idea.

Option 3: This option is incorrect. Fiona's idea moves away from the original online idea into phone calls to customers.

Case Study: Question 2 of 2

Question

Which statements best reflect why Ella's suggestion is effective?

Options:

1. It expands and improves on the original idea

2. It's feasible in the context of the organization

3. It replaces the original idea with a better, more realistic idea

4. It's unique

Answer:

Option 1: This option is correct. Online accounts will make the service more convenient for the customer. This element of Ella's suggested build meets the criteria for expanding on the original idea.

Option 2: This option is correct. Ella's idea fits with the organization's strategy of expanding its Web services.

Option 3: This option is incorrect. Ella's suggested build is an expansion of the original idea, not a replacement of it.

Option 4: This option is incorrect. The idea isn't necessarily unique, but it does expand nicely on the original idea and fits in well with the organization's Web strategy.

REFERENCES

References
1. **Creating an Innovative Culture** - 2002, Dennis Sherwood, Capstone Publishing
2. **The Creative Priority: Driving Innovative Business in the Real World** - 1998, Jerry Hirshberg, HarperBusiness
3. **Manager's Pocket Guide to Creativity** - 1998, Alexander Hiam, HDR Press
4. **The Concise Adair on Creativity and Innovation** - 2004, John Adair, Thorogood
5. **When Sparks Fly: Harnessing the Power of Group Creativity** - 1999, Dorothy Leonard and Walter Swap, Harvard Business Press

GLOSSARY

Glossary

A

analogy - When you say that something is like something else, for example: "The brain is like a computer." Analogies can be useful for helping to clarify and explain a creative or innovative idea, a process, or a procedure.

B

barrier - Something that gets in the way of or stifles creativity in an organization. The barriers may relate to people, resources, management, or organizational structure.

brainstorming - A technique for generating or "piling up" creative ideas developed in 1941 by the advertising executive Alex F. Osborn.

build - A process whereby coworkers add to each other's ideas.

C

creative block - When you can't generate new ideas any longer, or you stare at a blank piece of paper with no inspiration. You need to take action to help you move on to new ideas, and become creative again.

creative process - A five-stage model designed to guide creativity. The stages are research, generate, incubate, verify workability, and implement.

creativity - The ability to develop something new. It relates specifically to the art of being creative – seeing things in a new and different way.

E

extrovert - A person who is typically confident, gregarious, and outgoing. The introversion-extroversion scale has long been associated with personality testing and assessment. See also introvert.

H

hotdesking - When no one has a designated desk at work, but office space is used on a first come, first served basis. A team can come together for the duration of a project, and then disband again at the end.

I

incubation

Also known as hothousing, where your original idea is put aside for a time, before it is exposed to evaluation. This time lapse often allows variations to be found, and the idea to be built on, improving the quality of the initial proposal.

inertia

When the project stalls, then progress slows down, and eventually everything grinds to a halt. This may be due to problems with the leadership of a project – the leader may not be decisive enough, or have the confidence to make tough decisions. Alternatively, inertia may be the result of the team involved in the project.

innovation
Often the end result of being creative. When creative ideas are implemented, this results in innovation.

introvert
A person who is typically withdrawn, shy, and inward-looking. The introversion-extroversion scale has long been associated with personality testing and assessment. The theory was made popular by Hans Eysenck, and other psychologists. See also extrovert.

L

launch - The unveiling of a new product, idea, service, or innovation.

N

Nominal Group Technique - A highly structured team technique that is used for generating creative and innovative ideas. It was first developed by Andrew Delbecq and Andrew Van de Ven in 1971.

R

role playing - A creativity-boosting technique that involves the performing of imaginary roles, or the acting out of real-life situations. Role playing is often used to simulate real-life events.

S

sabotage - When an inventor deliberately or unintentionally ruins a creative project by stalling, withdrawing support for the idea or criticizing it, or being pessimistic.

V

visionary - A person who sets the vision, mission, and goals that the creative team should follow; gives a sense of purpose to others' creative efforts; is personally creative and thinks up ideas; and has the power to act and make key decisions.

W

Workable - Refers to an idea that addresses the identified need and supports the organization.

www.ingramcontent.com/pod-product-compliance
Lightning Source LLC
Chambersburg PA
CBHW020927180526
45163CB00007B/2916